MAMA NEEDS A DRINK

BY **TAGE LEE**

Illustrated by **VIVIAN MINEKER**

This book is dedicated to my husband Ryan,
who always gets Mama a drink.

"Morning, Mama!
Let's all start the day!"
"Not yet, sweetie.
It's too early to play."

"Wait in your bed until
seven, my dear.
It's way too soon
for this noise in my ears."

"But I want to jump,
and I want to shout!
Can we go to the park
and start running about?"

Mama has had it,
and jumps out of bed.
She says, "Put on your shoes,"
while she clutches her head.

"Oh! I dropped both my socks
in the toilet right there!"
"Oh no," grumbles Mama,
"Not your only good pair."

But she is far too tired
to wash socks in the sink.
What Mama needs most
is a really stiff drink.

"A beer would be good,
but Baileys will do.
In the coffee it goes."
One shot, and now two.

"Into the bright red wagon
all you crazy kids go.
Plus a Baileys and coffee
for Auntie in tow."

"I see all our friends
near the willow tree there!
Let's race!" shout the kids,
as they run without care.

In the park, the kids skip,
run, holler, and yell,
until Auntie says,
"Oh no! Someone fell!"

Another kid down!
Another kid weeping!
"I'm sorry, my baby,
please look before leaping!"

Mama kisses it better,
gives a smile and a wink.
"Oh boy," Auntie says,
"Do you need a stiff drink?"

"Baileys is good,
but rosé would be best."
Auntie pulls out a bottle
and says, "Let's de-stress."

So while into the cups
all the sweet rosé flows,
kids swing up and down,
and slide high to low.

Up onto the ladder they climb to the sky,
and skip rocks on the river and puddles nearby.

Into the sandbox
the littles all go,
rolling around,
like angels in snow.

Til one of them's shouting,
"There's sand in my eyes!
Get it out, get it out!"
as he screams, kicks, and cries.

"Now please use this water,
and blink, blink, blink, blink!"
"Oh boy," Mama says,
"looks like I need a drink."

"Rosé would be good,
but red wine is much better.
To the liquor store we go!
Kiddies, put on your sweaters!"

A Merlot, a Shiraz,
or a Malbec to choose?
"One of each!" chuckles Mama,
feeling highly amused.

Back to the house
go kids, wagon, and wine.
"But why?" say the littles.
"That was such a good time!"

"Because it's time to eat
and fill up with good food.
If not, you will both be
in super bad moods."

"Eat, eat, eat, eat, eat!
Fill your wee bellies up."
Gulp, gulp, gulp, gulp, gulp.
Mama refills her cup.

"It's not even dark out
and plates fill the sink.
Now you both need a nap
and I need a stiff drink."

"Into bed you will go
and fall swiftly asleep.
Mama hopes you are tired,
and don't make a peep."

"Have a good nap, my dears!"
is her exiting line,
as she puts up her feet and
gulps up her wine.

But naptime is short,
and the kids wake up fighting.
Mama's temper feels short.
"Stop your kicking and biting!"

It's almost time for supper
and Dadda must work late.
Good thing Auntie is
Mama's best dinner date.

While the kids all complain
that they hate cauliflower,
Auntie and Mama
drink strong whiskey sours.

"After a long day for all
let's raise our glasses 'til they clink
and make a toast, above all else,
to really, really good, stiff drinks!"

The End.

Thank you to Megan Williams, Vivian Mineker, and Kait DeWolff, for helping me create this book, without your help, none of this would have been possible.

A huge shout out to my amazing friends and family for being so supportive. An enthusiastic group of encouraging people is a powerful one.

Thank you to my daughter and fluctuating hormones for inspiring this book, as well as my husband Ryan and sister Kalee for all your love. Last but not least, thank you to my parents, John and Judy, who didn't think this idea was crazy and realized that they too always needed humour and a drink to get through raising us, "Harris Girls."

About the Author

Tage Lee lives with her husband and daughter in Vancouver, Canada. One of her favourite parts of being a Mama is exchanging honest stories of parenting with her friends.
In her spare time she loves to drink wine, rhyme, visit her family cabin in the woods, and travel (without kids).
Although it takes some convincing, she truly does love family time with or without a drink in hand.

About the Illustrator

Vivian Mineker is a Taiwanese American from Taipei and Portland. She works as a freelance illustrator specializing in watercolor and colored pencils, as well as digital.
She currently lives in Slovenia with her husband and mini goldendoodle, Darlie.